U.S. Department of Labor
Elaine L. Chao, Secretary

Occupational Safety and Health Administration
John L. Henshaw, Assistant Secretary

OSHA 3075
2002 (Revised)

OSHA will make this information available to sensory impaired individuals upon request. Call (202) 693–1999. The teletypewriter (TTY) number is (877) 889–5627.

Contents

Introduction

This booklet provides an overview of basic electrical safety on the job.

Electricity is essential to modern life, both at home and on the job. Some employees — engineers, electricians, electronic technicians, and power line workers, among them — work with electricity directly. Others, such as office workers and sales people, work with it indirectly. Perhaps because it has become such a familiar part of our daily life, many of us don't give much thought to how much our work depends on a reliable source of electricity. More importantly, we tend to overlook the hazards electricity poses and fail to treat it with the respect it deserves.

Why should you be concerned about electrical hazards?

Electricity has long been recognized as a serious workplace hazard, exposing employees to electric shock, electrocution, burns, fires, and explosions. In 1999, for example, 278 workers died from electrocutions at work, accounting for almost 5 percent of all on-the-job fatalities that year, according to the Bureau of Labor Statistics. What makes these statistics more tragic is that most of these fatalities could have been easily avoided.

What OSHA standards address electrical safety?

OSHA standards cover many electrical hazards in many different industries. OSHA's general industry electrical safety standards are published in *Title 29 Code of Federal Regulations (CFR)*, Part 1910.302 through 1910.308 — Design Safety Standards for Electrical Systems, and 1910.331 through 1910.335 — Electrical Safety-Related Work Practices Standards.

OSHA's electrical standards are based on the National Fire Protection Association Standards NFPA 70, *National Electric Code,* and NFPA 70E, *Electrical Safety Requirements for Employee Workplace*s.

OSHA also has electrical safety standards for the construction industry, in *29 CFR* 1926, Subpart K. OSHA's standards for marine terminals, in *29 CFR* 1917, and for longshoring, in *29 CFR* 1918, reference the general industry electrical standards in Subpart S of Part 1910. The shipyard standards, in *29 CFR* 1915, cover limited electrical safety work practices in *29 CFR* 1915.181.

Although OSHA operates a federal occupational safety and health program, 24 states and 2 territories operate their own OSHA-approved programs. In those states, the standards and other procedures governing electrical safety may not be identical to the federal requirements. They must, however, be at least as effective as the federal standards.

How do OSHA's standards minimize electrical hazards?

OSHA standards focus on the design and use of electrical equipment and systems. The standards cover only the exposed or operating elements of an electrical installation such as lighting, equipment, motors, machines, appliances, switches, controls, and enclosures, requiring that they be constructed and installed to minimize workplace electrical dangers. Also, the standards require that certain approved testing organizations test and certify electrical equipment before use in the workplace to ensure it is safe.

Electricity: The Basics

What affects the flow of electricity?

Electricity flows more easily through some materials than others. Some substances such as metals generally offer very little resistance to the flow of electric current and are called "conductors." A common but perhaps overlooked conductor is the surface or subsurface of the earth. Glass, plastic, porcelain, clay, pottery, dry wood, and similar substances generally slow or stop the flow of electricity. They are called "insulators." Even air, normally an insulator, can become a conductor, as occurs during an arc or lightning stroke.

How does water affect the flow of electricity?

Pure water is a poor conductor. But small amounts of impurities in water like salt, acid, solvents, or other materials can turn water itself and substances that generally act as insulators into conductors or better conductors. Dry wood, for example, generally slows or stops the flow of electricity. But when saturated with water, wood turns into a conductor. The same is true of human skin. Dry skin has a fairly high resistance to electric current. But when skin is moist or wet, it acts as a conductor. This means that anyone working with electricity in a damp or wet environment needs to exercise extra caution to prevent electrical hazards.

What causes shocks?

Electricity travels in closed circuits, normally through a conductor. But sometimes a person's body — an efficient conductor of electricity — mistakenly becomes part of the electric circuit. This can cause an electrical shock. Shocks occur when a person's body completes the current path with:

- both wires of an electric circuit;
- one wire of an energized circuit and the ground;
- a metal part that accidentally becomes energized due, for example, to a break in its insulation; or
- another "conductor" that is carrying a current.

When a person receives a shock, electricity flows between parts of the body or through the body to a ground or the earth.

What effect do shocks have on the body?

An electric shock can result in anything from a slight tingling sensation to immediate cardiac arrest. The severity depends on the following:

- the amount of current flowing through the body,
- the current's path through the body,
- the length of time the body remains in the circuit, and
- the current's frequency.

This table shows the general relationship between the amount of current received and the reaction when current flows from the hand to the foot for just 1 second.

Effects of Electric Current in the Human Body

Current	Reaction
Below 1 milliampere	Generally not perceptible
1 milliampere	Faint tingle
5 milliamperes	Slight shock felt; not painful but disturbing. Average individual can let go. Strong involuntary reactions can lead to other injuries.
6–25 milliamperes (women)	Painful shock, loss of muscular control*
9–30 milliamperes (men)	The freezing current or "let-go" range.* Individual cannot let go, but can be thrown away from the circuit if extensor muscles are stimulated.
50–150 milliamperes	Extreme pain, respiratory arrest, severe muscular contractions. Death is possible.
1,000–4,300 milliamperes	Rhythmic pumping action of the heart ceases. Muscular contraction and nerve damage occur; death likely.
10,000 milliamperes	Cardiac arrest, severe burns; death probable

* If the extensor muscles are excited by the shock, the person may be thrown away from the power source.

Source: W.B. Kouwenhoven, "Human Safety and Electric Shock," *Electrical Safety Practices*, Monograph, 112, Instrument Society of America, p. 93. November 1968.

What kind of burns can a shock cause?

Burns are the most common shock-related injury. An electrical accident can result in an electrical burn, arc burn, thermal contact burn, or a combination of burns.

Electrical burns are among the most serious burns and require immediate medical attention. They occur when electric current flows through tissues or bone, generating heat that causes tissue damage.

Arc or flash burns result from high temperatures caused by an electric arc or explosion near the body. These burns should be treated promptly.

Thermal contact burns are caused when the skin touches hot surfaces of overheated electric conductors, conduits, or other energized equipment. Thermal burns also can be caused when clothing catches on fire, as may occur when an electric arc is produced.

In addition to shock and burn hazards, electricity poses other dangers. For example, arcs that result from short circuits can cause injury or start a fire. Extremely high-energy arcs can damage equipment, causing fragmented metal to fly in all directions. Even low-energy arcs can cause violent explosions in atmospheres that contain flammable gases, vapors, or combustible dusts.

Why do people sometimes "freeze" when they are shocked?

When a person receives an electrical shock, sometimes the electrical stimulation causes the muscles to contract. This "freezing" effect makes the person unable to pull free of the circuit. It is extremely dangerous because it increases the length of exposure to electricity and because the current causes blisters, which reduce the body's resistance and increases the current.

The longer the exposure, the greater the risk of serious injury. Longer exposures at even relatively low voltages can be just as dangerous as short exposures at higher voltages. Low voltage does not imply low hazard.

In addition to muscle contractions that cause "freezing," electrical shocks also can cause involuntary muscle reactions. These reactions can result in a wide range of other injuries from collisions or falls, including bruises, bone fractures, and even death.

What should you do if someone "freezes" to a live electrical contact?

If a person is "frozen" to a live electrical contact, shut off the current immediately. If this is not possible, use boards, poles, or sticks made of wood or any other nonconducting materials and safely push or pull the person away from the contact. It's important to act quickly, but remember to protect yourself as well from electrocution or shock.

How can you tell if a shock is serious?

A severe shock can cause considerably more damage than meets the eye. A victim may suffer internal hemorrhages and destruction of tissues, nerves, and muscles that aren't readily visible. Renal damage also can occur. If you or a coworker receives a shock, seek emergency medical help immediately.

What is the danger of static electricity?

Static electricity also can cause a shock, though in a different way and generally not as potentially severe as the type of shock described previously. Static electricity can build up on the surface of an object and, under the right conditions, can discharge to a person, causing a shock. The most familiar example of this is when a person reaches for a door knob or other metal object on a cold, relatively dry day and receives a shock.

However, static electricity also can cause shocks or can just discharge to an object with much more serious consequences, as when friction causes a high level of static electricity to build up at a specific spot on an object. This can happen simply through handling plastic pipes and materials or during normal operation of rubberized drive or machine belts found in many worksites. In these cases, for example, static electricity can potentially discharge when sufficient amounts of flammable or combustible substances are located nearby and cause an explosion. Grounding or other measures may be necessary to prevent this static electricity buildup and the results.

Protection Against Electrical Hazards

What is the best way to protect yourself against electrical hazards?

Most electrical accidents result from one of the following three factors:

- unsafe equipment or installation,

- unsafe environment, or

- unsafe work practices.

Some ways to prevent these accidents are through the use of insulation, guarding, grounding, electrical protective devices, and safe work practices.

What protection does insulation provide?

Insulators such as glass, mica, rubber, or plastic used to coat metals and other conductors help stop or reduce the flow of electrical current. This helps prevent shock, fires, and short circuits. To be effective, the insulation must be suitable for the voltage used and conditions such as temperature and other environmental factors like moisture, oil, gasoline, corrosive fumes, or other substances that could cause the insulator to fail.

How do you identify different types of insulation?

Insulation on conductors is often color coded. Insulated equipment grounding conductors usually are either solid green or green with yellow stripes. Insulation covering grounded conductors is generally white or gray. Ungrounded conductors, or "hot wires," often are black or red, although they may be any color other than green, white, or gray.

Before connecting electrical equipment to a power source, it's a good idea to check the insulation for any exposed wires for possible defects. Insulation covering flexible cords such as extension cords is particularly vulnerable to damage.

The insulation that covers conductors in non-construction applications is regulated by Subpart S of *29 CFR* 1910.302 through 1910.308, *Wiring Design and Protection*. Subpart S generally requires insulation on circuit conductors. It also specifies that the insulation used should be suitable for the voltage and conditions. Conductors used in construction applications are regulated by Subpart K of *29 CFR* 1926.402 through 1926.408.

What is guarding and what protection does it offer?

Guarding involves locating or enclosing electric equipment to make sure people don't accidentally come into contact with its live parts. Effective guarding requires equipment with exposed parts operating at 50 volts or more to be placed where it is accessible only to authorized people qualified to work with it. Recommended locations are a room, vault, or similar enclosure; a balcony, gallery, or elevated platform; or a site elevated 8 feet (2.44 meters) or more above the floor. Sturdy, permanent screens also can serve as effective guards.

Conspicuous signs must be posted at the entrances to electrical rooms and similarly guarded locations to alert people to the electrical hazard and to forbid entry to unauthorized people. Signs may contain the word "Danger," "Warning," or "Caution," and beneath that, appropriate concise wording that alerts people to the hazard or gives an instruction, such as "Danger/High Voltage/Keep Out."

What is grounding and what protection does it offer?

"Grounding" a tool or electrical system means intentionally creating a low-resistance path that connects to the earth. This prevents the buildup of voltages that could cause an electrical accident.

Grounding is normally a secondary protective measure to protect against electric shock. It does not guarantee that you won't get a shock or be injured or killed by an electrical current. It will, however, substantially reduce the risk, especially when used in combination with other safety measures discussed in this booklet.

29 CFR, Part 1910.304, Subpart S, *Wiring Design and Protection,* requires at times a service or system ground and an equipment ground in non-construction applications.

A *service* or *system ground* is designed primarily to protect machines, tools, and insulation against damage. One wire, called the "neutral" or "grounded" conductor, is grounded. In an ordinary low-voltage circuit, the white or gray wire is grounded at the generator or transformer and at the building's service entrance.

An *equipment ground* helps protect the equipment operator. It furnishes a second path for the current to pass through from the tool or machine to the ground. This additional ground safeguards the operator if a malfunction causes the tool's metal frame to become energized. The resulting flow of current may activate the circuit protection devices.

What are circuit protection devices and how do they work?

Circuit protection devices limit or stop the flow of current automatically in the event of a ground fault, overload, or short circuit in the wiring system. Well-known examples of these devices are fuses, circuit breakers, ground-fault circuit interrupters, and arc-fault circuit interrupters.

Fuses and *circuit breakers* open or break the circuit automatically when too much current flows through them. When that happens, fuses melt and circuit breakers trip the circuit open. Fuses and circuit breakers are designed to protect conductors and equipment. They prevent wires and other components from overheating and open the circuit when there is a risk of a ground fault.

Ground-fault circuit interrupters, or GFCIs, are used in wet locations, construction sites, and other high-risk areas. These devices interrupt the flow of electricity within as little as 1/40 of a second to prevent electrocution. GFCIs compare the amount of current going into electric equipment with the amount of current returning from it along the circuit conductors. If the difference exceeds 5 milliamperes, the device automatically shuts off the electric power.

Arc-fault devices provide protection from the effects of arc-faults by recognizing characteristics unique to arcing and by functioning to deenergize the circuit when an arc-fault is detected.

What work practices help protect you against electrical hazards?

Electrical accidents are largely preventable through safe work practices. Examples of these practices include the following:

- deenergizing electric equipment before inspection or repair,
- keeping electric tools properly maintained,
- exercising caution when working near energized lines, and
- using appropriate protective equipment.

Electrical safety-related work practice requirements for general industry are detailed in Subpart S of *29 CFR* Part 1910, in Sections 1910.331–1910.335. For construction applications, electrical safety-related work practice requirements are detailed in Subpart K of *29 CFR* Part 1926.416 to 1926.417.

How can you protect yourself against metal parts that become energized?

A break in an electric tool's or machine's insulation can cause its metal parts to become "hot" or energized, meaning that they conduct electricity. Touching these energized parts can result in an electrical shock, burn, or electrocution. The best way to protect yourself when using electrical tools or machines is to establish a low-resistance path from the device's metallic case to the ground. This requires an equipment grounding conductor, a low-resistance wire that directs unwanted current directly to the ground. A properly installed grounding conductor has a low resistance to ground and greatly reduces the amount of current that passes through your body. Cord and plug equipment with a three-prong plug is a common example of equipment incorporating this ground conductor.

Another form of protection is to use listed or labeled portable tools and appliances protected by an approved system of double insulation or its equivalent. Where such a system is employed, it must be marked distinctively to indicate that the tool or appliance uses an approved double insulation system.

How can you prevent an accidental or unexpected equipment startup?

Proper lockout/tagout procedures protect you from the dangers of the accidental or unexpected startup of electrical equipment and are required for general industry by OSHA Standard 1910.333, *Selection and Use of Work Practices*. Requirements for construction applications are in *29 CFR* 1926.417, *Lockout and Tagging of Circuits*. These procedures ensure that electrical equipment is deenergized before it is repaired or inspected and protects you against electrocution or shock.

The first step before beginning any inspection or repair job is to turn the current off at the switch box and padlock the switch in the OFF position. This applies even on so-called low-voltage circuits. Securely tagging the switch or controls of the machine or equipment being locked out of service clarifies to everyone in the area which equipment or circuits are being inspected or repaired.

Only qualified electricians who have been trained in safe lockout procedures should maintain electrical equipment. No two of the locks used should match, and each key should fit just one lock. In addition, one individual lock and key should be issued to each maintenance worker authorized to lock out and tag the equipment. All employees who repair a given piece of equipment should lock out its switch with an individual lock. Only authorized workers should be permitted to remove it.

How can you protect yourself from overhead power lines?

Before working under or near overhead power lines, ensure that you maintain a safe distance to the lines and, for very high-voltage lines, ground any equipment such as cranes that can become energized. If working on power lines, ensure that the lines have been deenergized and grounded by the owner or operator of the lines. Other protective measures like guarding or insulating the lines help prevent accidental contact.

Employees unqualified to work with electricity, as well as mechanical equipment, should remain at least 10 feet (3.05 meters) away from overhead power lines. If the voltage is more than 50,000 volts, the clearance increases by 4 inches (10 centimeters) for each additional 10,000 volts.

When mechanical equipment is operated near overhead lines, employees standing on the ground should avoid contact with the equipment unless it is located outside the danger zone. When factoring the safe standoff distance, be sure to consider the equipment's maximum reach.

What protection does personal equipment offer?

Employees who work directly with electricity should use the personal protective equipment required for the jobs they perform. This equipment may include rubber insulating gloves, hoods, sleeves, matting, blankets, line hose, and industrial protective helmets designed to reduce electric shock hazard. All help reduce the risk of electrical accidents.

What role do tools play?

Appropriate and properly maintained tools help protect workers against electric hazards. It's important to maintain tools regularly because it prevents them from deteriorating and becoming dangerous. Check each tool before using it. If you find a defect, immediately remove it from service and tag it so no one will use it until it has been repaired or replaced.

When using a tool to handle energized conductors, check to make sure it is designed and constructed to withstand the voltages and stresses to which it has been exposed.

What special training do employees need?

All employees should be trained to be thoroughly familiar with the safety procedures for their particular jobs. Moreover, good judgment and common sense are integral to preventing electrical accidents. When working on electrical equipment, for example, some basic procedures to follow are to:

- deenergize the equipment,
- use lockout and tag procedures to ensure that the equipment remains deenergized,
- use insulating protective equipment, and
- maintain a safe distance from energized parts.

What's the value of a safety and health program in controlling electrical hazards?

Every good safety and health program provides measures to control electrical hazards. The measures suggested in this booklet should be helpful in establishing such a program. The responsibility for this program should be delegated to someone with a complete knowledge of electricity, electrical work practices, and the appropriate OSHA standards for installation and performance.

Everyone has the right to work in a safe environment. Safety and health add value to your business and your workplace. Through cooperative efforts, employers and employees can learn to identify and eliminate or control electrical hazards.

How Can OSHA Help Me?

OSHA can provide extensive help through a variety of programs, including assistance about safety and health programs, state plans, workplace consultations, voluntary protection programs, strategic partnerships, training and education, and more.

How does safety and health program management assistance help employers and employees?

Working in a safe and healthful environment can stimulate innovation and creativity and result in increased performance and higher productivity.

To assist employers and employees in developing effective safety and health programs, OSHA published recommended *Safety and Health Program Management Guidelines* (*Federal Register* 54(18):3904–3916, January 26, 1989). These voluntary guidelines can be applied to all worksites covered by OSHA.

The guidelines identify four general elements that are critical to the development of a successful safety and health management system:

- management leadership and employee involvement,
- worksite analysis,
- hazard prevention and control, and
- safety and health training.

The guidelines recommend specific actions under each of these general elements to achieve an effective safety and health program. The *Federal Register* notice is available online at www.osha.gov.

What are state plans?

State plans are OSHA-approved job safety and health programs operated by individual states or territories instead of Federal OSHA. The *Occupational Safety and Health Act of 1970 (OSH Act)* encourages states to develop and operate their own job safety and health plans and permits state enforcement of OSHA standards if the state has an approved plan. Once OSHA approves a state plan, it funds 50 percent of the program's operating costs. State plans must provide standards and enforcement programs, as well as voluntary compliance activities, that are at least as effective as those of Federal OSHA.

There are 26 state plans: 23 cover both private and public (state and local government) employment, and 3 (Connecticut, New Jersey, and New York) cover only the public sector. For more information on state plans, see the listing at the end of this publication, or visit OSHA's website at www.osha.gov.

How can consultation assistance help employers?

In addition to helping employers identify and correct specific hazards, OSHA's consultation service provides free, onsite assistance in developing and implementing effective workplace safety and health management systems that emphasize the prevention of worker injuries and illnesses.

Comprehensive consultation assistance provided by OSHA includes a hazard survey of the worksite and an appraisal of all aspects of the employer's existing safety and health management system. In addition, the service offers assistance to employers in developing and implementing an effective safety and health management system. Employers also may receive training and education services, as well as limited assistance away from the worksite.

Who can get consultation assistance and what does it cost?

Consultation assistance is available to small employers (with fewer than 250 employees at a fixed site and no more than 500 corporatewide) who want help in establishing and maintaining a safe and healthful workplace.

Funded largely by OSHA, the service is provided at no cost to the employer. Primarily developed for smaller employers with more hazardous operations, the consultation service is delivered by state governments employing professional safety and health consultants. No penalties are proposed or citations issued for hazards identified by the consultant. The employer's only obligation is to correct all identified serious hazards within the agreed-upon correction time frame.

Can OSHA assure privacy to an employer who asks for consultation assistance?

OSHA provides consultation assistance to the employer with the assurance that his or her name and firm and any information about the workplace will not be routinely reported to OSHA enforcement staff.

Can an employer be cited for violations after receiving consultation assistance?

If an employer fails to eliminate or control a serious hazard within the agreed-upon time frame, the consultation project manager must refer the situation to the OSHA enforcement office for appropriate action. This is a rare occurrence, however, because employers request the service for the expressed purpose of identifying and fixing hazards in their workplaces.

Does OSHA provide any incentives for seeking consultation assistance?

Yes. Under the consultation program, certain exemplary employers may request participation in OSHA's Safety and Health Achievement Recognition Program (SHARP). Eligibility for participation in SHARP includes, but is not limited to, receiving a full-service, comprehensive consultation visit, correcting all identified hazards, and developing an effective safety and health management system.

Employers accepted into SHARP may receive an exemption from programmed inspections (not complaint or accident investigation inspections) for a period of 1 year initially, or 2 years upon renewal. For more information concerning consultation assistance, see the consultation directory at the end of this publication, contact your regional or area OSHA office, or visit OSHA's website at www.osha.gov.

What is the Voluntary Protection Program?

Voluntary Protection Programs (VPPs) represent one part of OSHA's effort to extend worker protection beyond the minimum required by OSHA standards. VPP — along with onsite consultation services, full-service area offices, and OSHA's Strategic Partnership Program (OSPP) — represents a cooperative approach which, when coupled with an effective enforcement program, expands worker protection to help meet the goals of the *OSH Act*.

How does the Voluntary Protection Program work?

There are three levels of VPPs: Star, Merit, and Demonstration. All are designed to do the following:

- recognize employers who have successfully developed and implemented effective and comprehensive safety and health management systems;

- encourage these employers to continuously improve their safety and health management systems;

- motivate other employers to achieve excellent safety and health results in the same outstanding way; and

- establish a relationship between employers, employees, and OSHA that is based on cooperation.

How does VPP help employers and employees?

VPP participation can mean the following:

- reduced numbers of worker fatalities, injuries, and illnesses;

- lost-workday case rates generally 50 percent below industry averages;

- lower workers' compensation and other injury- and illness-related costs;

- improved employee motivation to work safely, leading to a better quality of life at work;

- positive community recognition and interaction;

- further improvement and revitalization of already good safety and health programs; and

- a positive relationship with OSHA.

How does OSHA monitor VPP sites?

OSHA reviews an employer's VPP application and conducts a VPP onsite evaluation to verify that the safety and health management systems described are operating effectively at the site. OSHA conducts onsite evaluations on a regular basis, annually for participants at the Demonstration level, every 18 months for Merit, and every 3 to 5 years for Star. Each February, all participants must send a copy of their most recent annual evaluation to their OSHA regional office. This evaluation must include the worksite's record of injuries and illnesses for the past year.

Can OSHA inspect an employer who is participating in the VPP?

Sites participating in VPP are not scheduled for regular, programmed inspections. OSHA handles any employee complaints, serious accidents, or significant chemical releases that may occur at VPP sites according to routine enforcement procedures.

Additional information on VPP is available from OSHA national, regional, and area offices, listed at the end of this booklet. Also, see **Outreach** on OSHA's website at www.osha.gov.

How can a partnership with OSHA improve worker safety and health?

OSHA has learned firsthand that voluntary, cooperative partnerships with employers, employees, and unions can be a useful alternative to traditional enforcement and an effective way to reduce worker deaths, injuries, and illnesses. This is especially true when a partnership leads to the development and implementation of comprehensive workplace safety and health management system.

What is OSHA's Strategic Partnership Program (OSPP)?

OSHA Strategic Partnerships are alliances among labor, management, and government to foster improvements in workplace safety and health. These partnerships are voluntary, cooperative relationships between OSHA, employers, employee representatives, and others such as trade unions, trade and professional associations, universities, and other government agencies. OSPPs are the newest member of OSHA's family of cooperative programs.

What do OSPPs do?

These partnerships encourage, assist, and recognize the efforts of the partners to eliminate serious workplace hazards and achieve a high level of worker safety and health. Whereas OSHA's Consultation Program and VPP entail one-on-one relationships between OSHA and individual worksites, most strategic partnerships seek to have a broader impact by building cooperative relationships with groups of employers and employees.

Are there different kinds of OSPPs?

There are two major types:

* comprehensive, which focus on establishing comprehensive safety and health management systems at partnering worksites; and

* limited, which help identify and eliminate hazards associated with worker deaths, injuries, and illnesses, or have goals other than establishing comprehensive worksite safety and health programs.

OSHA is interested in creating new OSPPs at the national, regional, and local levels. OSHA also has found limited partnerships to be valuable. Limited partnerships might address the elimination or control of a specific industry hazard.

What are the benefits of participation in the OSPP?

Like VPP, OSPP can mean the following:

- fewer worker fatalities, injuries, and illnesses;

- lower workers' compensation and other injury- and illness-related costs;

- improved employee motivation to work safely, leading to a better quality of life at work and enhanced productivity;

- positive community recognition and interaction;

- development of or improvement in safety and health management systems; and

- positive interaction with OSHA.

For more information about this program, contact your nearest OSHA office or go to the agency website at www.osha.gov.

Does OSHA have occupational safety and health training for employers and employees?

Yes. The OSHA Training Institute in Des Plaines, IL, provides basic and advanced training and education in safety and health for federal and state compliance officers, state consultants, other federal agency personnel, and private-sector employers, employees, and their representatives.

Institute courses cover diverse safety and health topics including electrical hazards, machine guarding, personal protective equipment, ventilation, and ergonomics. The facility includes classrooms, laboratories, a library, and an audiovisual unit. The laboratories contain various demonstrations and equipment, such as power presses, woodworking and welding shops, a complete industrial ventilation unit, and a sound demonstration laboratory. More than 57 courses dealing with subjects such as safety and health in the construction industry and methods of compliance with OSHA standards are available for personnel in the private sector.

In addition, OSHA's 73 area offices are full-service centers offering a variety of informational services such as personnel for speaking engagements, publications, audiovisual aids on workplace hazards, and technical advice.

For more information on grants, training, and education, write: OSHA Training Institute, Office of Training and Education, 1555 Times Drive, Des Plaines, IL 60018; call (847) 297-4810; or see **Outreach** on OSHA's website at www.osha.gov.

Does OSHA give money to organizations for training and education?

OSHA awards grants through its Susan Harwood Training Grant Program to nonprofit organizations to provide safety and health training and education to employers and workers in the workplace. The grants focus on programs that will educate workers and employers in small business (fewer than 250 employees), training workers and employers about new OSHA standards or about high-risk activities or hazards. Grants are awarded for 1 year and may be renewed for an additional 12 months depending on whether the grantee has performed satisfactorily.

OSHA expects each organization awarded a grant to develop a training and/or education program that addresses a safety and health topic named by OSHA, recruit workers and employers for the training, and conduct the training. Grantees are also expected to follow up with people who have been trained to find out what changes were made to reduce the hazards in their workplaces as a result of the training.

Each year OSHA has a national competition that is announced in the *Federal Register* and on the Internet at www.osha.gov/dte/sharwood/index.html.
If you do not have access to the Internet, you can contact the OSHA Office of Training and Education, 1555 Times Drive, Des Plaines, Illinois 60018, (847) 297–4810, for more information.

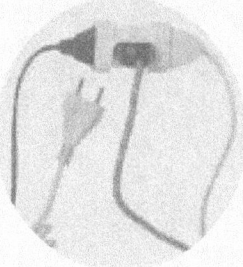

Does OSHA have other assistance materials available?

OSHA has a variety of materials and tools available on its website at www.osha.gov. These include e-Tools such as Expert Advisors and Electronic Compliance Assistance Tools (e-CATs), Technical Links, regulations, directives, publications, videos, and other information for employers and employees. OSHA's software programs and compliance assistance tools walk you through challenging safety and health issues and common problems to find the best solutions for your workplace. OSHA's comprehensive publications program includes more than 100 titles to help you understand OSHA requirements and programs.

OSHA's CD-ROM includes standards, interpretations, directives, and more and can be purchased on CD-ROM from the U.S. Government Printing Office. To order, write to the Superintendent of Documents, U.S. Government Printing Office, Washington, DC 20402, or phone (202) 512–1800. Specify OSHA Regulations, Documents and Technical Information on CD-ROM (ORDT), GPO Order No. S/N 729-013-00000-5.

What do I do in case of an emergency? Or if I need to file a complaint?

To report an emergency, file a complaint, or seek OSHA advice, assistance, or products, call (800) 321–OSHA or contact your nearest OSHA regional or area office listed at the end of this publication. The teletypewriter (TTY) number is (877) 889–5627.

You can also file a complaint online and obtain more information on OSHA federal and state programs by visiting OSHA's website at www.osha.gov.

OSHA Offices

Region I
(CT,* ME, MA, NH, RI, VT*)
JFK Federal Building, Room E340
Boston, MA 02203
(617) 565-9860

Region II
(NJ,* NY,* PR,* VI*)
201 Varick Street, Room 670
New York, NY 10014
(212) 337-2378

Region III
(DE, DC, MD,* PA,* VA,* WV)
The Curtis Center
170 S. Independence Mall West
Suite 740 West
Philadelphia, PA 19106-3309
(215) 861-4900

Region IV
(AL, FL, GA, KY,* MS, NC,* SC,* TN*)
SNAF
61 Forsyth Street SW, Room 6T50
Atlanta, GA 30303
(404) 562-2300

Region V
(IL, IN,* MI,* MN,* OH, WI)
230 South Dearborn Street, Room 3244
Chicago, IL 60604
(312) 353-2220

Region VI
(AR, LA, NM,* OK, TX)
525 Griffin Street, Room 602
Dallas, TX 75202
(214) 767-4731 or 4736 x224

Region VII
(IA,* KS, MO, NE)
City Center Square
1100 Main Street, Suite 800
Kansas City, MO 64105
(816) 426-5861

Region VIII
(CO, MT, ND, SD, UT,* WY*)
1999 Broadway, Suite 1690
PO Box 46550
Denver, CO 80202-5716
(303) 844-1600

Region IX
(American Samoa, AZ,* CA,* HI, NV,* Northern Mariana Islands)
71 Stevenson Street, Room 420
San Francisco, CA 94105
(415) 975-4310

Region X
(AK,* ID, OR,* WA*)
1111 Third Avenue, Suite 715
Seattle, WA 98101-3212
(206) 553-5930

---

* These states and territories operate their own OSHA-approved job safety and health programs. (Connecticut, New Jersey and New York plans cover public employees only.) States with approved programs must have a standard that is identical to, or at least as effective as, the federal standard.

OSHA Area Offices

Alabama

U.S. Department of Labor—OSHA
Vestavia Village, 2047 Canyon Road
Birmingham, AL 35216–1981
(205) 731-1534

U.S. Department of Labor—OSHA
3737 Government Boulevard, Suite 100
Mobile, AL 36693-4309
(251) 441-6131

Alaska

U.S. Department of Labor—OSHA
301 W. Northern Lights Blvd, Suite 407
Anchorage, AK 99503
(907) 271-5152

Arizona

U.S. Department of Labor—OSHA
3221 North 16th Street, Suite 100
Phoenix, AZ 85016
(602) 640-2348

Arkansas

U.S. Department of Labor—OSHA
TCBY Building, Suite 450
425 West Capitol Avenue
Little Rock, AR 72201
(501) 324-6291(5818)

California

U.S. Department of Labor—OSHA
5675 Ruffin Road, Suite 330
San Diego, CA 92123
(619) 557-5909

U.S. Department of Labor—OSHA
101 El Camino Plaza, Suite 105
Sacramento, CA 95815
(916) 566-7471

Colorado

U.S. Department of Labor—OSHA
1391 Speer Boulevard, Suite 210
Denver, CO 80204-2552
(303) 844-5285

U.S. Department of Labor—OSHA
7935 East Prentice Avenue, Suite 209
Greenwood Village, CO 80111-2714
(303) 843-4500

Connecticut

U.S. Department of Labor—OSHA
1057 Broad Street, Fourth Floor
Bridgeport, CT 06604
(203) 579-5581

U.S. Department of Labor—OSHA
Federal Building
450 Main Street, Room 613
Hartford, CT 06103
(860) 240-3152

Delaware

U.S. Department of Labor—OSHA
Caleb Boggs Federal Building
844 N King Street, Room 2209
Wilmington, DE 19801-3319
(302) 573-6518

Florida

U.S. Department of Labor—OSHA
8040 Peters Road, Building H-100
Fort Lauderdale, FL 33324
(954) 424-0242

U.S. Department of Labor—OSHA
Ribault Building, Suite 227
1851 Executive Center Drive
Jacksonville, FL 32207
(904) 232-2895

U.S. Department of Labor—OSHA
5807 Breckenridge Parkway, Suite A
Tampa, FL 33610-4249
(813) 626-1177

Georgia

U.S. Department of Labor—OSHA
450 Mall Boulevard, Suite J
Savannah, GA 31406
(912) 652-4393

U.S. Department of Labor—OSHA
2400 Herodian Way, Suite 250
Smyrna, GA 30080-2968
(770) 984-8700

U.S. Department of Labor—OSHA
LaVista Perimeter Office Park
2183 N. Lake Parkway
Building 7, Suite 110
Tucker, GA 30084-4154
(770) 493-6644/6742/8419

Idaho

U.S. Department of Labor—OSHA
1150 North Curtis Road, Suite 201
Boise, ID 83706
(208) 321-2960

Illinois

U.S. Department of Labor—OSHA
1600 167th Street, Suite 9
Calumet City, IL 60409
(708) 891-3800

U.S. Department of Labor—OSHA
O'hara Plaza
701 Lee Street, Suite #950
Des Plaines, IL 60016
(847) 803-4800

U.S. Department of Labor—OSHA
11 Executive Drive, Suite 11
Fairview Heights, IL 62208
(618) 632-8612

U.S. Department of Labor—OSHA
365 Smoke Tree Business Park
North Aurora, IL 60542
(630) 896-8700

U.S. Department of Labor—OSHA
2918 West Willow Knolls Road
Peoria, IL 61614
(309) 671-7033

Indiana

U.S. Department of Labor—OSHA
46 East Ohio Street, Room 453
Indianapolis, IN 46204
(317) 226-7290

Iowa

U.S. Department of Labor—OSHA
210 Walnut Street, Room 815
Des Moines, IA 50309
(515) 284-4794

Kansas

U.S. Department of Labor—OSHA
217 W. 3rd Street North
Room #400
Wichita, KS 67202
(316) 269-6644

Kentucky

U.S. Department of Labor—OSHA
John C. Watts Federal Building
330 W. Broadway, Room 108
Frankfort, KY 40601-1922
(502) 227-7024

Louisiana

U.S. Department of Labor—OSHA
9100 Bluebonnet Centre Boulevard
Suite 201
Baton Rouge, LA 70809
(225) 389-0474 (0431)

Maine

U.S. Department of Labor—OSHA
202 Harlow Street, Room 211
Bangor, ME 04401
(207) 941-8177

U.S. Department of Labor—OSHA
West Tower
100 Middle Street, Suite 410 West
Portland, ME 04101
(207) 780-3178

Maryland

U.S. Department of Labor—OSHA
1099 Winterson Road, Suite 140
Linthicum, MD 21090-2218
(410) 865-2055/2056

Massachusetts

U.S. Department of Labor—OSHA
639 Granite Street, 4th Floor
Braintree, MA 02184
(617) 565-6924

U.S. Department of Labor—OSHA
Valley Office Park
13 Branch Street
Methuen, MA 01844
(617) 565-8110

U.S. Department of Labor—OSHA
1441 Main Street, Room 550
Springfield, MA 01103-1493
(413) 785-0123

Michigan

U.S. Department of Labor—OSHA
801 South Waverly Road, Suite 306
Lansing, MI 48917-4200
(517) 322-1814

Minnesota

U.S. Department of Labor—OSHA
300 South 4th Street, Room 1205
Minneapolis, MN 55415
(612) 664-5460

Mississippi

U.S. Department of Labor—OSHA
3780 I-55 North, Suite 210
Jackson, MS 39211-6323
(601) 965-4606

Missouri

U.S. Department of Labor—OSHA
6200 Connecticut Avenue, Suite 100
Kansas City, MO 64120
(816) 483-9531

U.S. Department of Labor—OSHA
911 Washington Avenue, Room 420
St. Louis, MO 63101
(314) 425-4249

Montana

U.S. Department of Labor—OSHA
2900 4th Avenue North, Suite 303
Billings, MT 59101
(406) 247-7494

Nebraska

U.S. Department of Labor—OSHA
Overland–Wolf Building
6910 Pacific Street, Room 100
Omaha, NE 68106
(402) 221-3182

Nevada

U.S. Department of Labor—OSHA
705 North Plaza, Room 204
Carson City, NV 89701
(775) 885-6963

New Hampshire

U.S. Department of Labor—OSHA
279 Pleasant Street, Suite 201
Concord, NH 03301
(603) 225-1629

New Jersey

U.S. Department of Labor—OSHA
1030 St. Georges Avenue
Plaza 35, Suite 205
Avenel, NJ 07001
(732) 750-3270

U.S. Department of Labor—OSHA
500 Route 17 South, 2nd Floor
Hasbrouck Heights, NJ 07604
(201) 288-1700

U.S. Department of Labor—OSHA
Marlton Executive Park, Building 2
701 Route 73 South, Suite 120
Marlton, NJ 08053
(856) 757-5181

U.S. Department of Labor—OSHA
299 Cherry Hill Road, Suite 304
Parsippany, NJ 07054
(973) 263-1003

New York

U.S. Department of Labor—OSHA
401 New Karner Road, Suite 300
Albany, NY 12205-3809
(518) 464-4338

U.S. Department of Labor—OSHA
42-40 Bell Boulevard
Bayside, NY 11361
(718) 279-9060

U.S. Department of Labor—OSHA
5360 Genesee Street
Bowmansville, NY 14026
(716) 684-3891

U.S. Department of Labor—OSHA
201 Varick Street, Room #646
New York, NY 10014
(212) 337-2636

U.S. Department of Labor—OSHA
3300 Vickery Road
North Syracuse, NY 13212
(315) 451-0808

U.S. Department of Labor—OSHA
660 White Plains Road, 4th Floor
Tarrytown, NY 10591-5107
(914) 524-7510

U.S. Department of Labor—OSHA
1400 Old Country Road, Room 208
Westbury, NY 11590
(516) 334-3344

North Carolina

U.S. Department of Labor—OSHA
Century Station Federal Office Building
300 Fayetteville Street Mall, Room 438
Raleigh, NC 27601-9998
(919) 856-4770

North Dakota

U.S. Department of Labor—OSHA
1640 East Capitol Avenue
Bismark, ND 58501
(701) 250-4521

Ohio

U.S. Department of Labor—OSHA
36 Triangle Park Drive
Cincinnati, OH 45246
(513) 841-4132

U.S. Department of Labor—OSHA
Federal Office Building
1240 East 9th Street, Room 899
Cleveland, OH 44199
(216) 522-3818

U.S. Department of Labor—OSHA
Federal Office Building
200 North High Street, Room 620
Columbus, OH 43215
(614) 469-5582

U.S. Department of Labor—OSHA
420 Madison Avenue
Suite 600
Toledo, OH 43604
(419) 259-7542

Oklahoma

U.S. Department of Labor—OSHA
55 North Robinson, Suite 315
Oklahoma City, OK 73102-9237
(405) 278-9560

Oregon

U.S. Department of Labor, OSHA
Federal Office Building
1220 Southwest 3rd Avenue, Room 640
Portland, OR 97204
(503) 326-2251

Pennsylvania

U.S. Department of Labor—OSHA
850 North 5th Street
Allentown, PA 18102
(610) 776-0592

U.S. Department of Labor—OSHA
3939 West Ridge Road, Suite B12
Erie, PA 16506-1887
(814) 833-5758

U.S. Department of Labor—OSHA
Progress Plaza
49 North Progress Avenue
Harrisburg, PA 17109
(717) 782-3902

U.S. Department of Labor—OSHA
U.S. Custom House, Room 242
Second and Chestnut Streets
Philadelphia, PA 19106-2902
(215) 597-4955

U.S. Department of Labor—OSHA
Federal Office Building
1000 Liberty Avenue, Room 1428
Pittsburgh, PA 15222-4101
(412) 395-4903

U.S. Department of Labor—OSHA
Steigmaier
7 North Wilkes-Barre Boulevard, Suite 410
Wilkes-Barre, PA 18702-350
(570) 826-6538

Puerto Rico

U.S. Department of Labor—OSHA
Triple SSS Plaza Building
1510 F. D. Roosevelt Avenue, Suite 5B
Guaynabo, PR 00968
(787) 277-1560

Rhode Island

U.S. Department of Labor—OSHA
Federal Office Building
380 Westminster Mall, Room 543
Providence, RI 02903
(401) 528-4669

South Carolina

U.S. Department of Labor—OSHA
1835 Assembly Street, Room 1468
Columbia, SC 29201-2453
(803) 765-5904

Tennessee

U.S. Department of Labor—OSHA
2002 Richard Jones Road, Suite C-205
Nashville, TN 37215-2809
(615) 781-5423

Texas

U.S. Department of Labor—OSHA
903 San Jacinto Boulevard, Suite 319
Austin, TX 78701
(512) 916-5783 (5788)

U.S. Department of Labor—OSHA
Wilson Plaza
606 N. Carancahua, Suite 700
Corpus Christi, TX 78476
(361) 888-3420

U.S. Department of Labor—OSHA
8344 East R.L. Thornton Freeway, Suite 420
Dallas, TX 75228
(214) 320-2400 (2558)

U.S. Department of Labor—OSHA
700 E San Antonio St.
Room C-408
El Paso, TX 79901
(915) 534-6251

U.S. Department of Labor—OSHA
North Starr II, Suite 302
8713 Airport Freeway
Fort Worth, TX 76180-7610
(817) 428-2470 (485-7647)

U.S. Department of Labor—OSHA
507 N. Sam Houston Parkway, Suite 400
Houston, TX 77060
(281) 591-2438 (2787)

U.S. Department of Labor—OSHA
17625 El Camino Real, Suite 400
Houston, TX 77058
(281) 286-0583/0584 (5922)

U.S. Department of Labor—OSHA
Federal Office Building
1205 Texas Avenue, Room 806
Lubbock, TX 79401
(806) 472-7681 (7685)

Utah

U.S. Depaartment of Labor—OSHA
160 E 300 South
Heber-Wells Building
P. O. Box 146650
Salt Lake City, UT 84114-6650
(801) 530-6901

Virginia

U.S. Department of Labor—OSHA
Federal Office Building
200 Granby Street, Room 614
Norfolk, VA 23510
(757) 441-3820

Washington

U.S. Department of Labor—OSHA
505 106th Avenue, NE, Suite 302
Bellevue, WA 98004
(206) 553-7520

West Virginia

U.S. Department of Labor—OSHA
405 Capitol Street
Suite 407
Charleston, WV 25301
(304) 347-5937

Wisconsin

U.S. Department of Labor—OSHA
1648 Tri Parkway
Appleton, WI 54914
(920) 734-4521

U.S. Department of Labor—OSHA
1310 West Clairmont Avenue
Eau Claire, WI 54701
(715) 832-9019

U.S. Department of Labor—OSHA
4802 E. Broadway
Madison, WI 53716
(608) 264-5388

U.S. Department of Labor—OSHA
Henry S. Reuss Building
310 W. Wisconsin Ave, Suite 1180
Milwaukee, WI 53203
(414) 297-3315

---

* For issues involving federal agencies or private companies
working for federal agencies in Arizona, California, Guam,
Hawaii, and Nevada, call the numbers listed. For issues
involving private or state government employers in these
states, refer to the appropriate state office in Arizona,
California, Hawaii, and Nevada.

States and Territories with OSHA-Approved Safety and Health Plans

Alaska

Commissioner
Alaska Department of Labor
1111 W. 8th Street, Room 308
P.O. Box 21149
Juneau, AK 99802-1149
(907) 465-2700

Arizona

Director
Industrial Commission of Arizona
800 W. Washington
Phoenix, AZ 85007
(602) 542-5795

California

Director
California Department of Industrial Relations
455 Golden Gate Avenue, 10th floor
San Francisco, CA 94102
(415) 703-5050

Connecticut

Commissioner
Connecticut Department of Labor
200 Folly Brook Boulevard
Wethersfield, CT 06109
(860) 263-6505

Hawaii

Director
Hawaii Department of Labor and Industrial Relations
830 Punchbowl Street
Honolulu, HI 96831
(808) 586-8844

Indiana

Commissioner
Indiana Department of Labor
State Office Building
402 West Washington Street, Room W195
Indianapolis, IN 46204
(317) 232-2378

Iowa

Commissioner
Iowa Division of Labor
1000 E. Grand Avenue
Des Moines, IA 50319
(515) 281-3447

Kentucky

Secretary
Kentucky Labor Cabinet
1047 U.S. Highway 127 South, Suite 4
Frankfort, KY 40601
(502) 564-3070

Maryland

Commissioner
Maryland Division of Labor and Industry
Department of Labor Licensing and Regulation
MOSH
1100 N. Eutaw Street, Room 613
Baltimore, MD 21201-2206
(410) 767-2215

Michigan

Director
Michigan Department of Consumer and Industry Services
P.O. Box 30643
7150 Harris Drive
Lansing, MI 48909
(517) 373-7230

Minnesota

Commissioner
Minnesota Department of Labor and Industry
443 Lafayette Road
St. Paul, MN 55155
(651) 284-5010

Nevada

Administrator
Nevada Division of Industrial Relations
400 West King Street, Suite 400
Carson City, NV 89703
(775) 684-7260

New Jersey

Commissioner
New Jersey Department of Labor
John Fitch Plaza — Labor Building
Market and Warren Streets
P.O. Box 110
Trenton, NJ 08625-0110
(609) 292-2975

New Mexico

Secretary
New Mexico Environment Department
1190 St. Francis Drive
P.O. Box 26110
Santa Fe, NM 87502
(505) 827-2850

New York

Commissioner
New York Department of Labor
W. Averell Harriman State Office
Building-12, Room 500
Albany, NY 12240
(518) 457-2741

North Carolina

Commissioner
North Carolina Department of Labor
4 West Edenton Street
Raleigh, NC 27601-1092
(919) 807-2900

Oregon

Administrator
Oregon Department of Consumer and Business Services
Occupational Safety and Health Division (OR-OSHA)
350 Winter Street, N.E. Room 430
Salem, OR 97310-3882
(503) 378-3272

Puerto Rico

Secretary
Puerto Rico Department of Labor and Human Resources
Prudencio Rivera Martinez Building
505 Munoz Rivera Avenue
Hato Rey, PR 00918
(787) 754-2119

South Carolina

South Carolina Department of Labor, Licensing and Regulation
Koger Office Park, Kingstree Building
110 Centerview Drive
P.O. Box 11329
Columbia, SC 29211
(803) 896-4300

Tennessee

Commissioner
Tennessee Department of Labor and Workforce Development
710 James Robertson Parkway
Andrew Johnson Tower
Nashville, TN 37243-0659
(615) 741-2582

Utah

Commissioner
Labor Commission of Utah
160 East 300 South Street, 3rd floor
P.O. Box 146650
Salt Lake City, UT 84111
(801) 530-6901

Vermont

Commissioner
Vermont Department of Labor and Industry
National Life Building, Drawer 20
120 State Street
Montpelier VT 05620-3401
(802) 828-2288

Virgin Islands

Commissioner
Virgin Islands Department of Labor
2203 Church Street
Christiansted, St. Croix, VI 00820-4660
(340) 773-1990

Virginia

Commissioner
Virginia Department of Labor and Industry
Powers-Taylor Building
13 South, 13th Street
Richmond, VA 23219
(804) 786-2377

Washington

Director
Washington Department of Labor and Industries
P.O. Box 44001
Olympia, WA 98504-4001
(360) 902-4200 (5430)

Wyoming

Administrator
Worker's Safety and Compensation
 Division (WSC)
Wyoming Department of Employment
Herschler Building, 2nd Floor East
122 West 25th Street
Cheyenne, WY 82002
(307) 777-7786

OSHA Onsite Consultation Offices

Alabama

Safety State Program University of Alabama
432 Martha Parham West
Post Office Box 870388
Tuscaloosa, AL 35487
(205) 348-3033

Alaska

Consultation Section
ADOL/AKOSH
3301 Eagle Street
Post Office Box 107022
Anchorage, AK 99510-7022
(907) 269-4957

Arizona

Consultation and Training
Division of Occupational Safety & Health
Industrial Commission of Arizona
800 West Washington
Phoenix, AZ 85007-9070
(602) 542-1695

Arkansas

OSHA Consultation
Arkansas Department of Labor
10421 West Markham
Little Rock, AR 72205
(501) 682-4522

California

CAL/OSHA Consultation Service
2424 Arden Way, Suite 410
Sacramento, CA 95825
(916) 263-2856

Colorado

Occupational Safety and Health Section
Colorado State University
133 Environmental Health Building
Fort Collins, CO 80523
(970) 491-6151

Connecticut

Division of Occupational Safety and Health
Connecticut Department of Labor
38 Wolcott Hill Road
Wethersfield, CT 06109
(860) 566-4550

Delaware

Occupational Safety and Health
Division of Industrial Affairs
Delaware Department of Labor
4425 North Market Street
Wilmington, DE 19802
(302) 761-8219

District of Columbia

Office of Occupational Safety and Health
D.C. Dept of Employment Services
950 Upshur Street, N.W.
Washington, DC 20011
(202) 541-3727

Florida

Director of Environmental Safety and Health
Environmental and Occupational Health
College of Public Health
4003 East Fowler Avenue
Tampa, FL 33617
(813) 974-9962

Georgia

Onsite Consultation Program
Georgia Institute of Technology
O'Keefe Building, Room 22
151 6th Street, N.W.
Atlanta, GA 30332-0837
(404) 894-2643

Guam

OSHA Onsite Consultation
Dept. of Labor, Government of Guam
107 F Street
Tiyam, GU 96931
9-1-(671) 475-1101

Hawaii

Consultation and Training Branch
Dept of Labor and Industrial Relations
830 Punchbowl Street
Honolulu, HI 96813
(808) 586-9100

Idaho

Safety and Health Consultation Program
Boise State University
Safety & Health Consultation Department
1910 University Drive
Boise, ID 83725
(208) 426-3283

Illinois

Illinois Onsite Consultation
Industrial Service Division
Department of Commerce and Community Affairs
State of Illinois Center, Suite 3-400
100 West Randolph Street
Chicago, IL 60601
(312) 814-2337

Indiana

Division of Labor
Bureau of Safety, Education and Training
Room W195
402 West Washington
Indianapolis, IN 46204-2287
(317) 232-2688

Iowa

Iowa Workforce Development Labor Services
Bureau of Consultation and Education
1000 East Grand Avenue
Des Moines, IA 50319
(515) 281-7629

Kansas

21D Consultation Program
Kansas Department of Human Resources
512 South West 6th Street
Topeka, KS 66603-3150
(785) 296-2551

Kentucky

Division of Education and Training
Kentucky Labor Cabinet
1047 U.S. Highway 127, South
Frankfort, KY 40601
(502) 564-6895

Louisiana

7(c)(1) Consultation Program
Louisiana Department of Labor
1001 N. 23rd Street, Room 421
Post Office Box 94040
Baton Rouge, LA 70804-9094
(225) 342-9601

Maine

Division of Industrial Safety
Maine Bureau of Labor Standards
Workplace Safety and Health Division
State House Station #45
Augusta, ME 04333-0045
(207) 624-6400

Maryland

MOSH Consultation Services
Attention: Ms. Colleen Ridler
312 Marshall Avenue Rm 600
Laurel, MD 20707
(410) 880-4970

Massachusetts

Division of Occupational Safety and Health
Department of Workforce Development
1001 Watertown Street
West Newton, MA 02165
(617) 727-3982

Michigan

Consultation Education and Training Division
Bureau of Safety and Regulation
Michigan Department of Consumer and Industry Services
7150 Harris Drive, Post Office Box 30643
Lansing, MI 48909-8143
(517) 322-1809

Minnesota

Department of Labor and Industry
Consultation Division
443 LaFayette Road North
Saint Paul, MN 55155
(651) 284-5060

Mississippi

Mississippi State University
Center for Safety and Health
106 Crosspark Drive, Suite C
Pearl, MS 39216
(601) 939-2047

Missouri

Onsite Consultation Program
Division of Labor Standards
Department of Labor and Industrial Relations
3315 West Truman Boulevard, Room 205
Post Office Box 449
Jefferson City, MO 65109
(573) 751-3403

Montana

Department of Labor and Industry
Bureau of Safety
Post Office Box 1728
Helena, MT 59624-1728
(406) 444-6418

Nebraska

Division of Safety and Labor Standards
Nebraska Department of Labor
State Office Building, Lower Level
301 Centennial Mall, South
Lincoln, NE 68509-5024
(402) 471-4717

Nevada

Safety Consultation and Training Section
Division of Industrial Relations
Department of Business and Industry
1301 North Green Valley Parkway
Henderson, NV 89074
(702) 486-9140

New Hampshire

New Hampshire
Department of Health and Human Services
Office of Community & Public Health
6 Hazen Drive
Concord, NH 03301-6527
(603) 271-2024

New Jersey

New Jersey Department of Labor
Division of Public Safety and
Occupational Safety and Health
225 E. State Street, 8th Floor West
P.O. Box 953
Trenton, NJ 08625-0953
(609) 292-3923

New Mexico

New Mexico Environment Dept
Occupational Health & Safety Bureau
525 Camino de los Marquez, Suite 3
Post Office Box 26110
Santa Fe, NM 87502
(505) 827-4230

New York

Division of Safety and Health
State Office Campus
Building 12, Room 168
Albany, NY 12240
(518) 457-2238

North Carolina

Bureau of Consultative Services
NC Department of Labor — OSHA Division
4 West Edenton Street
Raleigh, NC 27601-1092
(919) 807-2905

North Dakota

Division of Environmental Engineering
Room 304
1200 Missouri Avenue
Bismarck, ND 58504
(701) 328-5188

Ohio

On-Site Consultation Program
Bureau of Occupational Safety and Health
LAWS Division/Ohio Department of Commerce
50 W. Broad Street, Suite 2900
Columbus, OH 43215
(614) 644-2631

Oklahoma

Oklahoma Department of Labor
OSHA Division
4001 North Lincoln Boulevard
Oklahoma City, OK 73105-5212
(405) 528-1500

Oregon

Oregon OSHA
Department of Consumer and Business Services
350 Winter Street, N.E., Room 430
Salem, OR 97301-3882
(503) 378-3272

Pennsylvania

Indiana University of Pennsylvania
Room 210, Walsh Hall
302 E. Walk
Indiana, PA 15705-1087
(724) 357-2396

Puerto Rico

Occupational Safety and Health Office
Department of Labor and Human Resources
21st Floor
505 Munoz Rivera Avenue
Hato Rey, PR 00918
(787) 754-2171

Rhode Island

OSHA Consultation Program
Division of Occupational Health and Radiation Control
Rhode Island Department of Health
3 Capital Hill, Room 206
Providence, RI 02908
(401) 222-2438

South Carolina

South Carolina Department of Labor, Licensing and Regulation
3600 Forest Drive
Post Office Box 11329
Columbia, SC 29204
(803) 734-9614

South Dakota

Engineering Extension
Onsite Technical Division
SD State University, West Hall
Box 510, 907 Harvey Dunn Street
Brookings, SD 57007
(605) 688-4101

Tennessee

OSHA Consultative Services Division
Tennessee Department of Labor
3rd Floor
710 James Robertson Parkway
Nashville, TN 37243-0659
(615) 741-7036

Texas

Workers' Health and Safety Division
Workers' Compensation Commission
Southfield Building
4000 South I H 35
Austin, TX 78704
(512) 804-4640

Utah

State of Utah Labor Commission
Workplace Safety and Health
Consultation Services
160 East 300 South
Salt Lake City, UT 84111
(801) 530-6901

Vermont

Division of Occupational Safety and Health
Vermont Department of Labor and Industry
National Life Building, Drawer #20
Montepilier, VT 05620-3401
(802) 828-2765

Virginia

Virginia Department of Labor and Industry
Occupational Safety and Health
Training and Consultation
13 South 13th Street
Richmond, VA 23219
(804) 786-6359

Virgin Islands

Division of Occupational Safety and Health
Virgin Islands Department of Labor
3021 Golden Rock
Christiansted St. Croix, VI 00840
(809) 772-1315

Washington

Washington Dept of Labor and Industries
Division of Industrial Safety and Health
Post Office Box 44643
Olympia, WA 98504
(360) 902-5638

West Virginia

West Virginia Department of Labor
Capitol Complex Building #6
Room 319
Charleston, WV 25305
(304) 558-7890

Wisconsin (Health)

Wisconsin Department of Health and Family Services
Division of Health
Bureau of Occupational Health
1 West Wilson Street, Room B157
PO Box 2659
Madison, WI 53701-2659
(608) 266-9383

Wisconsin (Safety)

Wisconsin Safety Consultation
N14W23833 Stone Ridge Drive, Suite B100
Waukesha, WI 53188-1125
(262) 523-3044

Wyoming

Wyoming Department of Employment
Workers' Safety and Compensation Division
Herschler Building, 2 East
122 West 25th Street
Cheyenne, WY 82002
(307) 777-7786

To report an emergency, file a complaint, or seek OSHA advice, assistance, or products, call (800) 321-OSHA or contact your nearest OSHA regional or area office. The teletypewriter (TTY) number is (877) 889-5627.

www.ingramcontent.com/pod-product-compliance
Lightning Source LLC
Chambersburg PA
CBHW051817170526
45167CB00005B/2056